a taste of **tea**

a taste of tea

Brian Glover

photography by Diana Miller

RYLAND
PETERS
& SMALL

LONDON NEW YORK

Senior Designer Sonya Nathoo
Senior Editors Miriam Hyslop and
Catherine Osborne
Location Research Jess Walton
Production Manager Patricia Harrington
Publishing Director Alison Starling

Photographer Diana Miller
Stylist Liz Belton

First published in the United Kingdom
in 2007 by Ryland Peters & Small, Inc.
519 Broadway, 5th Floor
New York, NY 10012
www.rylandpeters.com

10 9 8 7 6 5 4 3 2 1

Text © Brian Glover 2007

Design and photographs copyright
© Ryland Peters & Small 2007

ISBN-10: 1-84597-473-5
ISBN-13: 978-1-84597-473-2
Printed and bound in China.

Library of Congress Cataloging-
in-Publication Data

Glover, Brian, 1958-
 A taste of tea / Brian Glover ;
photography by Diana Miller.
   p. cm.
 Includes index.
 ISBN 978-1-84597-473-2
 1. Cookery (Tea) 2. Tea. I. Title.
 TX817.T3G56 2007
 641.6'372--dc22

2007015937

To Nana, who always loved her tea

contents

introduction   6

tea essentials   8

tea around the world   26

suppliers   62

index   64

introduction

There is an amazing variety of teas available, produced by countries all over the world. The wealth of choice is so great it can be bewildering. Finding out a little more about a drink that's enjoyed worldwide, but still taken for granted by many, is what this book is all about.

Tea has traveled far from its origins on remote Chinese mountainsides. No other drink has such deep-rooted social importance in so many different parts of the globe. From informal gatherings of family and friends, to ritualized ceremonies and rarefied tea tastings, tea's place in society and affections is surely unique. So whether you are interested in the differences between green teas, Oolongs, and Keemuns; unraveling the fascinating history of the "China drink;" or learning how tea can help you relax or stay healthy—this book has something for you.

tea essentials

Thank God for tea!

What would the world do without tea? How did it exist?

I am glad I was not born before tea.

Reverend Sydney Smith 1771–1845

the universal appeal of tea

For some of us tea is no more than a tea bag in a mug—a drink that's hastily gulped down as we rush to leave the house in the morning. For others it is well nigh a religion, celebrated in ceremonies in which every tiny detail has enormous significance. Whether you're a daily tea drinker or a tea connoisseur, there lies a world of tea for the tasting—from everyday teas that will make your daily cup a thing worth pausing for, to rare, highly-prized teas for you and your guests to savor sip by sip. There are teas for every kind of social occasion, as from its very beginnings drinking tea has always been about sitting down with others, to chat and gossip while the pot gets refreshed once, twice, and maybe more.

Tea can be highly individual, with blends to suit different moods and times of the day. Select from strong, dark-liquoring teas to kick-start you in the morning, to palely-loitering green teas to help you unwind at night. Alternatively, counter that mid-afternoon energy dip with a brisk, high-altitude Ceylon or lose yourself in a good book and a cup of fragrant Formosa Oolong. There are teas to take with a splash of milk and teas whose subtle aroma and taste you will want to savor all on their own.

Tea can come imbued with tradition and retro charm—when was the last time you sat down to rediscover the delights of a proper Afternoon Tea? You can also make it cutting-edge by serving a rare, exquisite white tea or an organic first-flush Darjeeling from a tea garden in the foothills of the lofty Himalayas. Tea is what and how you make it—whether that be a highly personal indulgence or a shared joy.

origins

Tea in China One of the most appealing stories surrounding the origins of tea tells how the Emperor Shen Nung fell asleep under a tea bush while he was boiling some water, when a leaf from the bush dropped into his pot. On waking, the Emperor found the new drink deliciously bittersweet, restorative, and curiously stimulating.

Whatever the truth behind the myth, the story of tea had begun. By the time the scholar Lu Yu wrote his *Cha Jing* (a treatise on tea) in the Tang Dynasty (circa AD 780), tea-drinking in China was a centuries-old tradition, especially in Buddhist monasteries and among the nobility.

Tea houses have a long and venerable history in China as places where men (rarely women) met to make music, declaim poetry, and tell tall tales. With the Cultural Revolution of the 1960s, these tea houses all but disappeared. However, in recent years, many Chinese cities and towns have re-established tea houses as places of culture and recreation.

Trade in tea beyond China China first traded tea with close neighbours Tibet, Korea, and Mongolia. However, it was the taking of tea to Japan by Buddhist monks (circa AD 730, then more enduringly in the late 12th century) that marked a crucial step in the history of tea outside China. The Japanese focus on the *Zen cha do* ("teaism" or the "Way of Tea"), gave the tea ceremony an elaborate philosophy and aesthetic, which gradually moved out of the monastery and into the home. By the 15th century, many households in Japan had their own tea house and women, rather than men, had a central role in the tea ceremony itself.

tea gains ground in the west

By repute at least, tea was known in Europe by the beginning of the 17th century. In 1618 Czar Michael Fedorovich received a gift of tea from the Chinese, which marked the beginning of tea's journey across the steppes and into the Russian soul. Soon after this, Portuguese and Dutch traders brought tea back to western Europe. It quickly became fashionable in Paris and tea was first sold in London in 1657. Diarist Samuel Pepys, ever one to keep up with the latest trend, recorded taking his first sip of tea in 1660. Tea's popularity in Britain was sealed when Catherine of Braganza married Charles II in 1662. As part of her dowry from Portugal she brought the important trading port of Bombay (now called Mumbai) and, crucially for our story, a box of tea. The royal connection made tea desirable. At first only the wealthy could afford it, but by the middle of the 18th century tea was popular among all classes of society. In 1784 the Comte de La Rochefoucauld was amazed to note that in "England the drinking of tea is general … the humblest peasant has his tea, just like the rich man." In 1700 just 20,000 pounds of tea was imported, by the end of the century it had reached a staggering 20 million pounds or 2 pounds for every man, woman, and child in the country. By 1871 that figure had doubled. Tea in America was not publicly available for sale until 1690, and it wasn't until after the Revolution was over in 1789 that the US entered the tea trade.

While tea triumphed in Britain, and became the national beverage in Ireland, Russia, and India, coffee held sway throughout most of Europe. Through trade, Britain took tea all over the world and nowadays, tea is popular in more parts of the world than at any point in its history.

trade in tea—past & present

The English East India Company imported its first cargo of China tea from the Chinese port of Amoy (known today as Xiamen) in 1669, and the company dominated the global trade in tea well into the 19th century. The world's tea trade and auctions centered on London, and the British imposed a tax on all tea imports to its colonies. It was the opposition against such taxes that led to the Boston Tea Party in 1773 and, eventually, the American War of Independence.

During this period, trade with China was not always easy and the British were keen to look for alternative sources for what had fast become their national drink. They eventually turned to India, where tea was found to grow well in the northeast regions of the country. The first British-grown Assam black tea was sold in London in the late 1830s. The tea gardens of Darjeeling, in the foothills of the Himalayas, were planted in the 1850s and from then on the British dependency on China teas diminished. The British took tea-growing to Sri Lanka in the 1860s and later to East Africa. Similarly, the Dutch established tea plantations in Indonesia.

Modern tea-trading Until the 20th century, Britain dominated the world trade in tea, but as more tea producing countries started to hold their own tea auctions this influence declined. Today, tea production is a huge global industry, much of it geared to quickly-brewed blends and easy-to-use tea bags. Despite this, the last two decades have seen a revival of interest in traditionally-made and organically-produced teas. Fair Trade initiatives are also helping smaller, more traditional growers and tea producers to become established in the market.

the language of tea

Where did the word "tea" come from? Trade had a significant influence on how the word traveled back to Europe. Tea was traded with the English and Dutch via the port of Amoy (modern-day Xiamen), where tea is known as *t'e* (pronounced "tay") in the region's local dialect. Countries that traded with the Dutch adopted the word giving us modern-day English tea, Dutch *tee*, French *thé*, and Spanish *te*. In some dialects of English, particularly in Ireland, tea is still pronounced "tay."

The Portuguese, however, traded with China via Macao where the Mandarin word for tea was (and still is) *ch'a*. Hence the Portuguese called tea *chá*. The Portuguese shipped tea via their colonies in India and as a result *chá* passed into Hindi as the word *chai* or *ca*. Centuries later, British servicemen serving in India picked up the Indian word *chai* and 'a cup of char' passed into colloquial English meaning a cup of good strong tea.

Tea is *cha* in Japanese and many of the items used in a traditional tea ceremony include the word *cha*, such as *chashitsu* (tea house), *chabana* (traditional flower arrangement), and *chasen* (the bamboo whisk used to make the tea). So highly-prized is tea in Japan that the word can be prefixed with an honorific "o," so that the full tea ceremony becomes the *ochaji*.

Incidentally, the word Pekoe, which is often used to describe fine leaf teas, is also of Chinese origin—coming from the Chinese word *bai-hao*, referring to the fine hairs on the youngest leaf buds of the tea bush. These leaves have a silvery velvet appearance and are reckoned to make the very finest teas of all.

growing, harvesting, & producing tea

The tea bush thrives at cool, high altitudes. How the bush is grown profoundly affects the finished flavor of your cup of tea. The soil it grows in, the altitude it is grown at, and the point at which the leaf tips are picked all play a part. Some tea bushes are specially shaded before harvesting to enhance the flavor of the finished tea. In other parts of the world, the climate causes the bushes to "flush"—put out new shoots—throughout the year. This means plucking can take place year-round. Whereas in some places, harvesting is strictly seasonal with experts distinguishing between first, second, or autumnal flushes. Tea harvesting, or plucking, is done by hand and is incredibly labor intensive. The pickers need to be skilled, using their judgment about which shoots are ready for picking.

In **orthodox** processing, the leaves are first withered to reduce their moisture levels, then rolled so that they bruise, and finally oxidized or "fermented" to develop their flavor. Drying or "firing" stops the fermentation process. In traditional tea production, the teas would be withered by exposure to the sun, bruised by "rattling" in a basket, hand-shaped, and then dried either over a fire or in the sun. Nowadays the majority of tea production is fully automated with rollers doing the bruising and the leaves fired in massive ovens.

The **Cut, Tear, and Curl** (CTC) method was invented in the mid-20th century and is usually employed for the finer end of the scale—fanning and dust grades. Instead of being rolled, the leaves are cut and torn. This speeds up the fermentation process and produces a lower grade of tea that is ideal for quick-brewing teas and tea bags.

making tea

If you want to buy fine teas, it's best to visit a small, specialty tea merchant. This will give you the opportunity to discuss your tea preferences with the staff, perhaps even have blends created to suit your own personal taste. Many specialist tea sellers will also arrange tea tastings. Once you know your teas, you can order specialty varieties via mail order and the internet. Buy your tea in small amounts and, most importantly, keep it dry. Tea will absorb moisture and other flavors quite easily, so keep your teas in airtight canisters or caddies, in a cool, dark place.

The paraphernalia of tea-making is part of its charm—teapots alone are infinitely collectable. Some of the most covetable are the traditional unglazed Jixing clay teapots from China. Also good are teapots with mesh baskets that allow you to remove the leaves once the tea has brewed. Some people claim you should never wash the inside of a teapot, as the patina adds flavor. It would certainly be sacrilegious to wash a Jixing pot in detergent.

Whether you opt for cups or mugs depends on the time of day and personal preference. It seems right to serve fine China teas in exquisite porcelain or celandon tea bowls or in the chunkier Japanese and Korean pottery versions. The Chinese Guywan tea bowl comes with its own saucer and lid, which keeps the tea warm through its multiple infusions.

A beautifully laid table for English afternoon tea (usually served at 5 o'clock) can be very seductive—complete with china or silver teapots, pastry forks, tiered vintage cake stands, and antique creamers (not forgetting sugar lumps and silver tongs for those who like sweet tea).

brewing the perfect cup of tea

Making a good cup of tea is a case of understanding how to get the best out of the particular type of tea you are using. No one rule covers all types of tea. While tea bags are convenient, the range and quality of loose-leaf teas is much greater. The best tea bags are the larger ones made of a nylon or fine cheesecloth mesh, which allow the tea leaves plenty of room to infuse. Since many teas, especially black teas, become harsh or bitter if the leaves are left to infuse too long in the water, teapots with removable infuser baskets are useful. Use filtered water if possible to avoid strong chemical flavors from faucet water that can affect the taste of delicate teas. And, always warm the pot first.

Black teas

๖ Estimate about 1 teaspoon of black leaf tea per person.

๖ Most smaller black leaf teas need around 2–3 minutes brewing time whereas larger leaf teas require up to 4 minutes.

Green & white teas

๖ These do not have to be made in a pot—they can be made very simply in an individual cup or tea bowl. Allow about half a teaspoon of green or white tea per cup or bowl.

๖ The finest green or white teas should be made with water that has cooled slightly from boiling point (175–185°F). Allow up to 4–5 minutes for the first infusion, and extra time for subsequent infusions. Fine Japanese teas brew more quickly in 1–2 minutes.

tea around the world

If man has no tea in him,

he is incapable of understanding truth and beauty.

(Japanese proverb)

china teas

Over the centuries, China has produced hundreds of different teas. Green tea is the most widely drunk in China, but it is for its black teas (also known as red teas) that China is most famous in the West.

Oolongs are halfway between black and green teas. They contain less caffeine than black teas, as they are only partly oxidized, and have a complex character with nutty, fruity aromas. The names of traditional Oolongs describe the shape of the leaves and are wonderfully poetic, such as *Da Hongpao* (Great Red Robe) and *Shoumei* (Old Man's Eyebrows).

Keemun teas are named after the area where they were first grown—Qimen in Anhui province —and were among the first teas brought to the West in the 17th century. Keemuns make a lovely golden tea with a warm, floral character.

Yunnan teas are quite special. Yunnan Pure Gold is made from only the young golden buds of the tea bush. They are complex teas with sweet, peppery, and smoky flavors.

Pu-erh teas are highly-prized and are also from the Yunnan province. These teas come compressed into bricks or small cakes. Like some wines, it is said that Pu-erh teas get better the longer they age. They have a bold, earthy taste and a deep red-brown color and are thought to reduce cholesterol and help in the digestion of fatty foods.

display teas

Display teas raise a simple drink to the level of high artistry. These special teas originated in the homes of Chinese aristocrats, and are made from high-quality, large leaf green or black teas that are hand-tied with silk thread or rolled to make shapes. When they are infused, these shapes unfurl to reveal exquisite flower or leaf-like forms, sometimes with unexpectedly colorful centers created from dried flower petals.

The addition of colorful flower petals also adds flavor to display teas. Chrysanthemum petals add sharpness, while jasmine, orange flower, or plum blossom give a perfumed sweetness. A few of the best known are:

๙ Green Peony (Lu Mudan)—unfurls to reveal a beautiful flower-like shape
๙ Green Lychee (Lu Lizi)—a tight bundle of green leaves made to resemble the lychee fruit
๙ Brocade of Flowers (Jin Shang Tian Hua)—has chrysanthemum petals tied inside
๙ Black Sea Anemone (Hong Mudan)—a rare, black display tea with a sweet flavor.

As well as these flower-like teas, display teas also include large leaf teas, rolled while damp, then dried so that they unfurl in the cup when hot water is added. Jade Rings, made from the first spring shoots; Jasmine Pearls, scented with jasmine petals; and Dragon Eye, which is made from one of best green teas, are among the best known.

These special teas deserve to be shown off. Make them in a glass pot or serve them individually in a heatproof glass or plain white Chinese tea bowl to display their exquisite shapes and colors.

names & labels

In the world of tea, the big division is between fermented and unfermented leaves. Confusingly, no real fermentation takes place, but the fresh leaves are bruised, then exposed to the air and so wilt and change color due to enzyme action. The process is correctly known as oxidation. Black teas are fully fermented/oxidized, green teas not at all, while yellow and Oolong teas undergo a partial oxidation.

Teas are graded, named, and labeled in many ways. China teas can be named by region, time of harvesting, the shape of the finished leaf, or by the legend they are associated with. In Darjeeling, India, teas are graded according to whether they come from the first "flush" (March/April) of new leaves or the second (May/June). Black teas are also graded by leaf size. A Flowery Orange Pekoe (FOP) means that the tea is made from the end bud and first two leaves of tender new shoots. A Tippy tea is one made up of a high proportion of the youngest and best golden leaf buds. Whereas a Souchong is a coarser grade of large leaf tea. A broken tea is a lesser grade, while the lowest grade of all is the fannings or dust left after the larger grades of leaf have been removed. These terms can be combined: so you might see the name Tippy Golden Flowery Orange Pekoe (or just the letters TGFOP) on a package, meaning a good, large leaf tea made with a high proportion of leaf tips.

A brisk tea describes the lively, fresh character of a tea that has been fired at the right point to stop the oxidation process. Teas are also split into light or dark liquoring teas, terms which refer to the color and strength of the finished brew.

white & yellow teas

White and yellow teas originate from the Fujian and Anhui provinces and are rare and very highly regarded, even in China. They produce light-colored infusions with subtle flavors.

White teas are made from the youngest, first-flush buds from selected tea bushes—so young that they are still covered in pale, silvery-white down or fine hairs, called the *bai-hao* (Anglicized as Pekoe). White teas are not fermented during processing. They are steamed after picking to prevent natural oxidation and then hand-rolled or shaped before drying. White teas contain minimal levels of caffeine and can also be brewed several times or for relatively lengthy periods without developing a bitter taste.

One of the best white teas, from Fuding in Fujian province, is known as Silver Tips or Needle (Baihao Yinzhen). In White Peony (Bai Mudan) tea, the steamed leaves are formed into little buds that expand when brewed. Fine white teas are now being produced in Darjeeling, India, and at the Kataboola Estate in Sri Lanka.

Yellow teas are also formed from young leaf buds, but they are allowed to dry for some hours in the sun. This drying allows a little natural oxidation to take place, giving yellow teas their deeper color and more definite, buttery taste. Yellow teas also have higher caffeine levels than white teas. Silver Needle (Jun Shan Yin Zhen) from the Jun Mountains in northern Fujian province, has rolled leaves that stand upright in the cup when infused, signifying good luck.

green teas

Green teas have been the most popular teas in China, Japan, and Korea for centuries. They have a lighter, more herbaceous flavor than black teas, contain less caffeine, and are rich in beneficial antioxidants.

Green teas are made from leaves picked at a slightly later stage than white and yellow teas. The leaves are processed without oxidation, but steamed or withered to preserve their natural green color and arrest enzyme action. The best Chinese green teas are still handcrafted, although the Japanese introduced mechanization into the production of their green teas as early as the 19th century.

Among the best known Chinese green tea in the West is Gunpowder Green or Green Pearl (Zu Cha), so-called because the leaves are rolled into pellets that look like gunshot, and Lucky Dragon (Young Hyson). One of the most famous, aristocratic, green teas is Dragon Well (Longjing) from Hangzhou in Zhejiang province with a mellow, nutty flavor.

The most esteemed Japanese green tea is Gyokuro, with large, deep green leaves, produced from bushes grown in the shade. But it is the finely powdered Matcha tea that is used in the Japanese tea ceremony. Matcha has a deep chlorophyll-green color and delivers quite a punch of flavor as the pulverization releases the maximum amount of minerals and caffeine. Sencha tea is made from the first-flush of leaves, so has a high mineral and vitamin content, and Genmaicha tea is mixed with roasted rice kernels to give it a toasted, nutty fragrance and flavor. Soba cha is made from roasted buckwheat, by itself or with green tea.

Japanese tea ceremony

More than any other drink or food, tea has, over the centuries, lent itself to rituals that carry immense socio-spiritual significance. In the Japanese tea ceremony—or *chaji*—this capacity reaches its symbolic and aesthetic peak.

The origins of the *chaji* are, like tea itself, Chinese. There are records of the Chinese introducing the Japanese to the ceremony of giving guests tea dating back almost 1200 years. The *chaji* is based on Zen Buddhist philosophy. A properly conducted *chaji* should represent a microcosm of the perfectly-ordered Zen universe and as a result, the ceremony is profoundly contemplative—each detail of the ceremony has a precise meaning.

Developed in the 15th century as a separate room surrounded by a garden, the Japanese tea house is dedicated entirely to the tea ceremony. The room is traditionally decorated with a seasonal flower arrangement, an appropriate symbolic wall-hanging, and a small fire for heating the water to make the tea. These elements of nature, art, and fire represent the most important features of the harmonious life. Traditionally, only one bowl (*chawan*) of Matcha green tea is prepared at a time to be ritualistically passed to each guest in turn by the host. In a full ceremony, this ritual is repeated three times.

Few modern Japanese homes have dedicated tea houses, but the tea ceremony remains a popular and important part of contemporary Japanese culture. Many Japanese attend *chaji* classes (in a variety of different schools of philosophy), taking turns being the host or the guests, and tea houses performing the ceremony are popular venues for family gatherings.

Indian teas

Indians love tea, especially taken strong, milky, and sweet. The finest teas are named after the area and estate where they are grown—with single-estate teas considered the very best of all.

Assam teas from northeast India are some of the strongest teas, characteristically described as having a malty sweetness and a smooth, rich flavor. Names of fine large leaf Assams to look out for are Tiraputi and Harmutty. Assam teas can easily turn bitter if the leaves are left to brew for too long and many people prefer to take Assam with milk.

Darjeeling is described as the "champagne of teas." Darjeelings grow in tea gardens at high altitudes in the foothills of the Himalayas. The bushes flush in two main spring seasons and are graded according to whether they are first or second flush—there is also sometimes an autumnal flush. Darjeelings tend to be medium strength and are often described as having a wine-like, muscatel flavor. The sweetness is balanced by a dry finish on the palate. Names of tea gardens to look out for are: Goomtee, Poobong (whose name translates as "valley beyond the clouds"), and Margaret's Hope. Some producers are experimenting with green Darjeelings.

The Nilgiri highlands lie in the southwest corner of India where the bushes can be picked all year round. Nilgiri teas are halfway between the powerful Assams and the delicate Darjeelings. They produce golden, fragrant teas that can be taken with or without milk. The Dunsandle organic estate is one of the best-regarded producers.

While China, India and Japan are the largest tea producers, the drink's popularity means that it's also grown in some quite unexpected places, such as the Tregothnan Estate in Cornwall, England, and at Sant' Andrea di Compito in Tuscany, Italy. Other areas include Georgia on the Black Sea, Nepal, and Malawi.

other tea producing countries

Three significant tea producers are Sri Lanka, Taiwan, and Kenya. Tea was introduced into Sri Lanka by the British in the 1860s and it is now a major producer. Often labeled Ceylon (the island's former name) teas, the best are grown at high altitudes, such as in Dimbula, Uva, and Nuwara Eliya.

Taiwanese teas are also better known by the island's former name—Formosa. Formosa Oolongs are considered by many to be among the very best teas in the world. Names to look out for are Tung Ting and Jade Oolong (Yu Oolong). Taiwan also produces unique Pouchong teas, which have a flavor often described as halfway between green and Oolong teas.

Kenya, where tea production really took off after Independence in the 1960s, is a major producer of strong black teas, much of it used in commercial blends and tea bags.

well-known & classic blends

Unless you seek out single-leaf teas, the chances are your tea will be blended. Some specialty blends were created so early in the marketing of tea that they have become classics.

Earl Grey Tea is the most famous blend. It originated in Britain where the eponymous lord was Prime Minister in the 1830s. Traditionally, Earl Grey is a medium-strength blend of black teas flavored with the oil of the Bergamot orange, but the flavor is so popular that nowadays you can also find Earl Grey green teas. Both Twinings and Jackson's of Piccadilly claim to have invented Earl Grey.

English Breakfast Tea produces a strong tea designed to kick-start your morning. Usually a blend of rich, malty Assams with brisk Ceylon teas, some brands add Kenya tea for depth of flavor. English breakfast tea is almost always taken with milk to mute its strength.

Russian Caravan is a delicious blend of black China teas—sometimes with Indian Darjeeling—that often has a slight smokiness from the addition of a little Lapsang Souchong. Perhaps fancifully, this blend is supposed to resemble the flavor of the tea transported from China to Russia via camel caravan in the 17th and 18th centuries.

Constant Comment Blend was created in the US in the 1940s by Ruth Bigelow and is still sold by the same company. It is a blend of black teas, dried orange zest, and sweet spices.

British afternoon tea

"… there are few hours in life more agreeable than the hour dedicated to the ceremony known as afternoon tea." *Portrait of a Lady* by Henry James

James' vision of tea on the summer lawn of an English country house, immortalized in numerous Merchant Ivory films, conjures up a quintessential image of Englishness. All Britain, it seems, once stopped to sip tea and nibble on a cucumber sandwich in the late afternoon. Even the French refer to afternoon tea as "Le Five O'clock." But, in Jane Austen's day, tea was drunk later in the evening, after an early dinner. As it became fashionable to dine later, "tea" was introduced as a meal to fill the gap between lunch and dinner. Anna, Duchess of Bedford, is credited as the first society hostess to serve her guests afternoon tea in the 1840s.

What makes the perfect Afternoon Tea? For many it must include light scones (like a rolled biscuit), jam (strawberry, damson or gooseberry), and thickly clotted Devonshire cream. In the north of England the scones may contain dried vine fruits, and be served with butter, not cream. A winter Afternoon Tea (cue a roaring log fire) might include buttered crumpets or cinnamon toast. Traditional cakes include Victoria sponge, moist fruitcake, and Battenburg.

British Afternoon Tea is undergoing a revival, especially in smart hotels, where a range of savory sandwiches, and scones, cream and preserves, and then cake are served—including such distinctly un-British items as éclairs, meringues, and chocolate gateaux cake. What would anglophile Henry James have made of that?

tea with food

For many, food with tea means cookies. To dunk or not to dunk? That is the question. Dunking may be frowned upon in polite society but it is widespread, nonetheless, and a hard habit to break. In Australia dunking is taken to a competitive level in the Tim Tam Slam in which the chocolate-filled cookie is used as a drinking straw for hot tea. He who drinks most before the cookie melts, wins. All a far cry from the sedate image of Marcel Proust dipping his madeleine into a cup of limeflower tea in a *Remembrance of Things Past*. Many people in the West (including the Chinese) also drink green tea—usually jasmine-scented—with meals in Chinese restaurants. But traditionally tea was rarely served with food in China. The exception is in Canton and Hong Kong where dim sum are eaten in tea houses accompanied by green tea.

Traditionally, in the north of England and Scotland, people drank tea with their evening meal—or High Tea—and many would still agree with Samuel Johnson, who described himself as "a hardened tea-drinker, who has for twenty years diluted his meals with only the infusion of this fascinating plant ..." (1757).

flavored teas

The most famous flower-scented tea is green Jasmine tea. Traditionally, dried jasmine petals are mixed with the green tea to give it a sweet, delicate flavor and balance out its astringency. Perhaps the most highly-esteemed jasmine tea is Jasmine Pearl, made by rolling large green leaf tea into small beads or pearls that are then infused with the powerfully scented blossoms. Black scented teas include Rose Congou (Meigui Hongcha) and orchid and chrysanthemum teas. Orange-blossom or dried sweet violet petals are sometimes added to black China teas.

In India, *chai masala* is very popular as a restorative drink—strong, milky tea is spiced with cardamom, ginger, cinnamon, and clove, and mace or nutmeg. It is served heavily sweetened.

It is very easy to make spice teas at home. Bury a few whole or lightly-crushed spices in a small canister with the tea, then leave them, tightly covered, for one to two weeks. Pieces of cut vanilla bean will deliciously perfume a light liquoring tea, or make your own winter spice blend by adding dried orange peel, clove and a cinnamon stick to a brisk Ceylon tea. For a simpler version, add a slice or two of fresh ginger, a pinch of dried elderflowers, or two to three lightly-bruised cardamom pods to a brewing pot of tea.

There are myriad modern, ready-mixed flavored teas; using either black or green teas as a base. Flavored Rooibos, Honeybush, and herbal teas are also popular. Favorites include fruit teas flavored with peach, apple, citrus, or berry fruits such as black currant or strawberry. Always check the labels of fruit teas, some include added sugar and can be very sweet.

tea in literature

"Love and scandal are the best sweeteners of tea." *Love in Several Masques* by Henry Fielding

There is a long tradition of writing about tea in China and Japan. Perhaps the most important book being by Lu Yu, who wrote the *Cha Jing* (a treatise on tea) circa AD 780. It gained a long-lasting reputation outside China as the definitive text on the art of making tea.

For European and American novelists of the 18th and 19th centuries, the tea table was a godsend. It was one of the few places in fiction (as in life) where women were allowed to be in charge. In the novels of Jane Austen, George Eliot, Charles Dickens, and many others, the men at such female-dominated occasions could be put at a disadvantage—often with comic, dramatic, and romantic results. Tea, when husbands were often absent, was also the time when news could be shared, flirting indulged in, and potential liaisons explored in forensic detail.

For American novelists Henry James and Edith Wharton, the occasion of tea was a chance to watch the openness of the New World collide with the finely-nuanced, social snobberies of old Europe. James was more than half in love with the Englishness of the ceremony of tea, but also recognized the subtle cruelties that could take place around the tea table.

At the Mad Hatter's tea party in *Alice's Adventures in Wonderland*, Lewis Carroll parodies the surface politeness of the English tea table by turning everything on its head: the hosts are openly rude to their "guest," Alice and, crucially, the worst possible faux-pas is committed—there is no tea. No society hostess would ever allow her table to run short of tea.

tea in the americas

Apart from that infamous Tea Party in Boston in 1773, tea in the US is renowned for the invention of iced tea at the 1904 St. Louis World's Fair by Richard Blechynden. Alcohol-laced tea punches had been around since the 18th century, but Blechynden was the first to see the potential of a non-alcoholic iced tea. Today, iced tea is popular worldwide—usually served over ice with lemon or lime wedges and herb sprigs such as mint or borage. A Long Island Iced Tea is quite a different kettle of fish—a potent cocktail invented in the 1970s and containing rum, vodka, triple sec, gin, tequila, and sour mix all diluted with cola. An American, Thomas Sullivan, also invented the tea bag, albeit inadvertently. As a tea merchant he sent out samples in small muslin bags. His customers used the bags as a convenient way to brew the tea and asked Sullivan for more. The tea bag was born.

Attempts were made to grow tea bushes on the island of Skidaway off the coast of Georgia as early as 1772, as a way of avoiding British taxes on tea imports. Today a small amount of tea is still produced at the Charleston Tea Plantation in South Carolina—they provide the tea drunk at the White House—and tea is probably more popular in the US now than at any point in its history.

As well as tea, South America also has its own indigenous infusion known as *maté* – prepared from the dried leaves of a type of holly—*Ilex paraguayensis*. *Maté* is a stimulating drink, containing moderately high levels of caffeine. *Chimarrão* is the high-roasted version popular in Brazil. *Maté* is traditionally drunk from a hollowed-out gourd also called a *maté*.

tea & health

From its earliest days in China, tea has been seen as having health-giving properties—
regarded as a bittersweet herb, linking yin and yang and so promoting well-being and
balance. Li Shizhen, a 16th-century herbalist wrote: "Tea clears the voice, gives brightness
to the eye, invigorates the body and refreshes the mind … it aids digestion, removes wind
and balances the temperature." A cure-all indeed.

When tea gained popularity in Britain, there was great debate on its effects on health.
Many social commentators were worried about its stimulating effect on the working classes
and those with nervous disorders. But in 1865 William Gladstone, the British prime minister,
echoed Li Shizhen when he claimed: "If you are cold, tea will warm you, if you are too heated,
it will cool you; if you are depressed, it will cheer [you up]."

Tea contains the stimulant caffeine. Black teas contain the highest levels, whereas white
and green teas contain the least. However, even black tea contains significantly less caffeine
than coffee, cup for cup. But, as the medieval Chinese herbalists claimed, tea also contains
chemicals which balance out the stimulating effects of the caffeine and modern research
suggests four cups of black tea a day will have a calming effect on stress levels in the body.
At a basic level, even the simple ritual of making and sipping tea can help you unwind.

Tea, particularly green tea, has antioxidant properties including tannins and plant phenols,
which work by scavenging for aging oxygen-derived, free-radicals in the blood. It is thought
that the polyphenolic antioxidant (catechin) can help prevent cancer and heart disease.

herbal teas, tisanes, & infusions

The leaves, flowers, or even berries of any edible plant can be used to make an infusion or tea. Some of the best-loved herbal infusions or tisanes have been valued for centuries for their effect on the body and spirit. Camomile aids sleep; Limeflower, made from the blossom of linden trees (*Tilia europea*), soothes, relaxes, and aids digestion; Ginger tea warms and strengthens the immune system; while Rosehip tea contains high levels of vitamin C and is good for warding off colds. Mint tea is popular after meals as it freshens the breath and aids good digestion. If you can obtain unsprayed herbs, fresh infusions are delicious and simple to make (see p60-1).

Rooibos (*Aspalathus linearis*) is a South African herb used to make an immensely popular tea. The young leaves and twigs of the bush are bruised, fermented, then dried. Rooibos contains significant amounts of minerals such as iron, potassium, zinc, and magnesium but is caffeine-free making it effective against headaches and hypertension. Rooibos is now also being processed as a "green," unfermented tea, with particularly high levels of antioxidants. Honeybush (*Cyclopia intermedia*), is another South African tea, made in the same way as Rooibos, which is naturally sweet, virtually caffeine-free, and also high in antioxidants.

Jiaogulan or Southern Ginseng (*Gynostemma pentaphyllum*) is a Chinese herb used to make an infusion that is popular in the Chinese province of Guizhou. It is naturally sweet and is rich in antioxidants that are thought to help fight against cell degeneration and aging.

herbal teas

Moroccan mint tea

In Morocco, tea is almost always served in small tea glasses and served sweet either after a meal or throughout the day. Experts insist that the correct mint to use is *Mentha longifolia* subsp. *schimperi* but you can use any mint.

Serves 4–6

1 tablespoon good green tea

large handful fresh mint, well-washed

brown sugar cubes, or golden granulated sugar,
*   to taste*

Put the tea into a large warmed pot or large French press and pack in the mint. Pour in 4 cups (900ml) just-off-the-boil water, stir, and infuse for 3–5 minutes. Choose a good tea that does not develop bitterness as it brews. Depress the plunger (if using a French press) and serve in small tea glasses sweetened with sugar.

Mint and cinnamon tea

Serve this in Moroccan tea glasses, giving each person a cinnamon stick to act as a stirrer.

Serves 4–6

cinnamon stick broken into 3 x 1-inch
(3 x 2.5-cm) lengths

large bunch fresh mint (about 2 ounces/50g),
*   well-washed*

four x 3- to 4-inch- (7.5- to 10-cm) long

cinnamon sticks, to serve

honey or brown sugar cubes, to taste

Put the cinnamon stick into the bottom of a large teapot or glass French press then pack in the mint. Pour in about 4 cups (900ml) boiling water and let it infuse for 5–6 minutes. Stir once, then depress the plunger (if using a French press). Otherwise strain into tea glasses and add a piece of cinnamon stick to each. Stir in sugar or honey to taste.

Ginger and lemongrass tea

A restorative infusion that's also warming. If you have any lemon balm or lemon verbena growing in the garden, a few leaves will reinforce the scent of the lemongrass. Make "stirrers" from a stalk of split lemongrass to release even more fragrance.

Serves 4

2- to 3-inch (5- to 7.5-cm) long piece fresh ginger, washed and cut into thick coin-shaped slices, unpeeled

2 stalks fresh lemongrass, tender basal parts only, plus extra to serve

a few lemon balm or lemon verbena leaves (optional)

honey or brown sugar cubes, to taste

Put the slices of ginger root in a warmed pot or French press, slice the lemongrass finely, and add to the pot along with the leaves if you are using. Pour in about 3 to 4 cups (750 to 900ml) boiling water, stir, and let it steep for 6-7 minutes. Strain and serve in glasses/cups with honey or brown sugar.

Thyme and honey tea

There is a huge choice of differently scented thymes around to grow, but lemon thyme (*Thymus x citrodorus*), is also widely available in stores. This tea is good for colds.

Serves 2

small bunch fresh lemon thyme

1–2 strips of organic unwaxed lemon or orange zest

2 coin-shaped slices fresh ginger, unpeeled

1–2 teaspoons honey per person, to taste

Place the thyme, lemon, or orange zest and ginger in a warmed glass teapot and add about 2½ cups (600ml) fresh boiling water. Stir, then let it steep for about 5–6 minutes. Strain and serve sweetened with honey.

suppliers

USA

Charleston Tea Plantation
6617 Maybank Highway
Wadmalow Island
SC 29487
USA
800-443-5987
www.biglowtea.com

Imperial Tea Court
1411 Powell Street
San Francisco
CA 94133
USA
800-547-5898 (toll-free in North
America)
www.imperialtea.com
*Teas and tea paraphernalia, including
Yixing teapots.*

Ito En
822 Madison Avenue
New York
NY 100021
USA
212-988-7111
www.itoen.com/store
*Specialist "high-end" Japanese, China,
and Indian teas.*

Samovar Tea Lounge
498 Sanchez Street
San Francisco
CA 94114
USA
415-626-4700
www.samovartea.com
Two tea lounges and online ordering.

Tea House
24260 Graver Lane
Naperville
IL 60564
USA
630-961-0877
www.theteahouse.com

Teaism, a teahouse
2009 R street NW
Washington, DC 20009
202 667-3827 or
877-883-2497
www.teaism.com

Ten Ren Tea
Head Office
419 Eccles Avenue
South San Francisco
CA 94080
USA
650-583-1047
www.tenren.com
*Specialists in Taiwanese, Chinese,
and Japanese teas. Stores throughout
North America and world, also mail
order via the internet.*

Upton Tea Imports
34a Hayden Rowe Street
Hopkinton
MA 01748
USA
800-234-8327 (toll-free in North
America)
www.uptontea.com
Huge range of teas to order online.

CANADA

China Tea House
350 Highway 7
Suite 211,
Chalmers Gate
Richmond Hill L4B 3N2
Ontario
Canada
905 882 9952

Tearoom T
1568 West Broadway
Vancouver BC
V6J 5K9
Canada
604-730-8390
www.tealeaves.com

Ten Ren
550 Main Street
Vancouver BC
V6A 2TG
Canada
604-684-1566
www.tenren.com
Several stores across Canada.

Van Cheong's Fine Teas
Unit 212
Lansdowne Centre
Richmond BC
V6X 2XG
Canada
604-279 1839
www.vancheong.com

index

A
afternoon tea, 47
America, 17, 55
antioxidants, 36, 56, 59
Assam tea, 17, 40

B
black teas: brewing, 25
  caffeine, 56
  fermentation, 32
  grading, 32
blends, 44
Boston Tea Party (1773),
  17, 55
brewing tea, 25
Buddhism, 13, 39
buying tea 22

C
caffeine, 28, 35, 36, 56, 59
canisters, 22
Catherine of Braganza, 14
Ceylon teas, 43
Charles II, King of England,
  14
China teas, 13, 28, 48, 52
  display teas, 31
  grades and names, 18,
  32
  serving, 13, 22
  trade, 14, 17
Constant Comment Blend,
  44
cups, 22

Cut, Tear, and Curl (CTC)
  method, 21

D
Darjeeling, 17, 32, 40
display teas, 31
dunking, 48
Dutch traders, 17, 18

E
Earl Grey Tea, 44
East India Company, 17
English Breakfast Tea, 44

F
fermentation, 21, 32
flavored teas, 51
flower petals, 31
food, tea with, 47, 48
Formosa Oolongs, 43
fruit teas, 51

G
ginger and lemongrass tea,
  61
grading teas, 32
green teas, 32, 36
  brewing, 25
  health benefits, 56
  serving, 48
growing tea, 21

H
harvesting tea, 21

health, 56
herbal teas, 59–61
Honeybush tea, 51, 59

I
iced tea, 55
India, 14, 17, 18, 40

J
Japan, 13, 18, 39, 48
Jasmine tea, 51
Jiaogulan tea, 59

K
Keemun teas, 28
Kenya, 43

L
language of tea, 18
literature, 52
London, 14, 17
Lu Yu, 13, 52

M
making tea, 22
maté, 55
mint and cinnamon tea, 60
mint tea, Moroccan, 60

N
Nilgiri teas, 40

O
Oolongs, 28, 32, 43

P
Pekoe teas, 18, 32, 35
processing leaves, 21
Pu-erh teas, 28

R
Roiboos tea, 51, 59
Russia, 14
Russian Caravan, 44

S
Souchongs, 32
South America, 55
spice teas, 51
Sri Lanka, 17, 43

T
Taiwan, 43
tea bags, 17, 25, 32, 55
tea bowls, 22
tea ceremony, 13, 18, 36,
  39
tea houses, 13, 39
teapots, 22, 25
thyme and honey tea, 61
trade, 13, 14, 17, 18

W
water, 25
white teas, 25, 35

Y
yellow teas, 32, 35
Yunnan teas, 28

acknowledgments

A special thank you to the Tea House, based in London, UK, for the loan of props for the photo shoot.

All background images taken from *Japanese Pattern*, published by Pepin Press.